21-DAY CONSECRATION

SET APART FOR THE MASTER'S USE

2 TIMOTHY 2:21 "Therefore, if anyone cleanses himself from the latter, he will be a vessel for honor, sanctified and useful for the Master, prepared for every good work."
NKJV

What People Are Saying
About Karon Y. Yarborough's

21-DAY CONSECRATION

SET APART FOR THE MASTER'S USE

"21-Day Consecration: Set Apart for the Master's Use" is a proactive, step-by-step guide to acknowledging and preparing yourself for service to God. The content and ability to journal your progress and what God may be speaking to you while reading is enriching and an insightful read."

Kimberly Young

"First allow me to say how amazed I was that I was actually bothered that I was only able to read a few pages. However, what I read was absolutely God ordained for me. You ever feel like you when you pick up something read that God selected it just for you. He met my needs in that moment and I was so grateful that Karon was a willing obedient vessel. I am sure everyone will get something different from this devotional. For Kara, I pray on a prayer call and for myself daily and I always remember to anoint myself. It's imperative for me to do before I go to the throne. So, thank you Karon from my spirit and my fleshly man."

Kara Young

Come out from among them and be ye separate —the road God has predestined for us everyone can't go—choosing to take this walk may sometimes be lonely and uncertain but the reward in beautifully purposed. This devotional will be a healing tool for the masses. Growing in the Lord is a beautiful journey this devotional is heaven sent just like the author congratulations and well done Sissy! I'm so excited to have a front seat to the birth of your bountiful gifts."

Sabrina Tucker

21-DAY CONSECRATION

SET APART FOR THE MASTER'S USE

2 TIMOTHY 2:21 "Therefore, if anyone cleanses himself from the latter, he will be a vessel for honor, sanctified and useful for the Master, prepared for every good work."
NKJV

Karon Y. Yarborough

21-DAY CONSECRATION SET APART FOR THE MASTER'S
*USE copyright © October 2021 **Karon Y. Yarborough***

All rights reserved. No part of this publication may be reproduced, stored in a retrieval system, or transmitted in any form by any means, electronic, mechanical, photocopy, recording, or otherwise, without the prior permission of the publisher, except as provided for by USA copyright law.

ISBN: 978-1-7352672-6-5

Published by Maximized Productions, LLC.

UPH Publishing Div.

6715 Suitland Rd. Morningside, MD 20746

www.maximizedproductions.com

Cover Design: Maximized Productions, LLC.

UPH Pub. Div.

Book Design by Dawn M. Harvey

Please direct your inquiries to the address above or visit:

Email: karonspeaksinfo@gmail.com

Or Follow Karon on Facebook, Twitter, and Instagram:

IG:	*karonspeaks*
FB:	*karonyarborough (Public)*
TWTR:	*karonspeaks*

PRINTED IN THE UNITED STATES OF AMERICA

FOREWORD

Minister Karon Yarborough has written a much needed and timely guide for the believer. Often times our busy schedules, our jobs, and our daily responsibilities consume all of our time. We become inundated with so many different things that sometimes we do not spend the appropriate time with God, necessary to build a covenant relationship. That is why this is such a worthy read.

This guide gives you all of the tools you need to develop a close and intimate relationship with God, or reconnect with God if you feel like you are off track. If you are a new believer, you will feel well equipped in your spiritual walk by utilizing the strategies Minister Karon has shared. And for anyone who feels disconnected, alone, or like you no longer hear your Father's voice the way you used to, this is exactly what you need.

The most precious relationship we will ever have is with God. When that relationship is primary it serves everything else in our lives. In a society where reverence for God appears diminished, it's important to remember that we are a peculiar people. God has called us to be Holy and Set Apart. It is important for us to allow the Holy Spirit and the Bible to help guide us into that sacred place of consecration. No matter where we are on our spiritual journey, we all need to consecrate ourselves to the Lord in order to deepen our personal knowledge of Christ and grow in our spiritual walk. This is just as important even if we've only just gotten saved, because consecration is the basis for every spiritual experience. And having an experience or encounter with God is what it is all about. And oh what a wonderful place to be. With our Heavenly Father, walking in sweet communion.

*"I exhort you therefore, brothers, through the compassions of God **to present your bodies a living sacrifice**, holy, well pleasing to God, which is your reasonable service." Romans 12:1*

Dr. Dawn M. Harvey, Pastor

Destiny International Christian Center

PREFACE

We are living in a time when people want something more than just an everyday human experience – the desire to feel something greater; do something greater; live in a mindset of something greater; and expecting God to do something greater. You feel like you are so different from others, but you can't pinpoint what it is that sets you apart. You have this longing to get more knowledge and understanding of Who God truly is. You have questions about your purpose and why you do or see things differently than others. How do we get there? How do we live in a space that is different than the mundane of everyday experiences?

You wake up; go to the bathroom to bathe; prepare breakfast for you and the family; get the kids ready for school; prepare yourself to leave to go to work; meet up with the same people at the office; attend several meetings about the work that you're supposed to get done but can't get done because you have another meeting immediately after the meeting that you're currently in; and then you get to your office, only to realize that you haven't eaten lunch and it's already 2 PM. So, what do you do? You go to the vending machine to get a snack to keep you fueled until time to leave at 5 PM. SURPRISE… You have just received another task from your supervisor, asking for your input on a report that was due 3 hours ago, so you will have to read immediately, in order for you to get it back to them before you leave for the day. Well, now it's 6 PM; and your scheduled time to leave has long passed, so, someone else is picking up your children and preparing dinner for them. When do you get the opportunity to settle down and get the experience that you long for? When do you have that encounter with God that you so desire? When do you have a chance to experience something greater or live in the moment of something greater? Have you got that "ah-huh" moment that has caused a paradigm shift in your mind of something greater? If you cannot answer these questions with confidence, it's time for you to settle down and let's work on spending some time with God for the next 21 days, consecrating ourselves to be set apart for the Master's use.

ACKNOWLEDGMENTS

Thank You Daddy (Yahweh) and Your Holy Spirit Who breathed the breath of life into this book. Without it, I nor this book would not be in existence. To my son who is near and dear to my heart. Many times you have no idea that you are the reason I kept living and pushing through.

Most gratitude to Rev. Sherry Barnes, who birthed out what was laying dormant within me.

To Minister Deborah Leaner who pushed me to see what you saw. Thank you for trusting me with what God gave you!

To Pastor Jenkins and First Lady Trina, you taught me so much about character, integrity and what it means to remain humble. Thank you for opportunities to share the Gospel through leadership.

To my publisher, Pastor Dawn, you have inspired and encouraged me when I didn't think my writing can make a difference. You have been patient and loving through it all. Words cannot express how much I love and appreciate the PUSH.

Pastor Nichole, I love you BIG for all that you are and how you love me!

To my Sistah Tribe and spiritual daughters, thank you for holding me accountable to get the book finished and submitted. You are the bestest!! LOL

CONTENTS

	Section	Page
1	Introduction Consecration	17
2	Times of Preparation	19
3	Praying Time	21
4	It's a Time of Fasting	23
5	The Anointing Oil Used for Consecration	25
6	The Sounds of Worship and Praise	28
7	Suggested Music Selection	33
8	Your Mouth Matters	35
9	The Altar Call	39
10	Rededication of Life in Christ	42
11	Unsure of Salvation	44
12	Devotions	46

INTRODUCTION CONSECRATION

For I am the LORD your God. You shall therefore consecrate yourselves, and you shall be holy; for I am holy. ~ Leviticus 11:44a

Are you beginning to feel like you want to be alone with God? Have you felt a deeper desire to read more of His Word? Are you feeling the need to stay in His presence? Has your worship experience grown stronger and deeper? These are all signs that God is calling you to a time of consecration.

There are times in our lives that God says to His chosen, it's time to pull away from the people of the world and set aside time to be alone with Him. In fact, He will change your appetite for the things of this world in a bid to prepare you to serve Him in a way that will be beyond your imagination (Ephesians 3:20). In preparation for the assignment for your life, there will be a pulling, a beckoning, a call, and a deep desire to get away from your day-to-day routine to spend time alone with Him. You might feel the urge to fast and spend more time in prayer. Reading your Bible and having study time is also one of the indications of the time of consecration.

During this time of consecration, God will draw you closer, sharpen your spirit of discernment, enable you to hear clearly, and receive direction and revelation from Him. He may also enlighten your spiritual eyes to see things you have never noticed before. This is so that you will know when He is showing you things for you to intercede on behalf of others; for you to become a watchman or gatekeeper on assignment to do spiritual warfare.

This is the time to lay aside worldly desires and focus on the desires of God. Salvation is not for us alone, but also for the lost that need to know Christ for themselves. You might be the person that God is calling to lead someone on a path toward salvation – the acceptance of Jesus Christ.

Be alert to how God directs you during this time of consecration. Others are waiting and relying on you to show them the way!

TIMES OF PREPARATION

Psalm 63:1

O God, You are my God; Early will I seek You; My soul thirsts for You; My flesh longs for You in a dry and thirsty land where there is no water.

*B*efore you exercise, it is imperative that you prepare your body for the movements that you will do during your regimen. I would suggest that you stretch and get your body relaxed and limber before doing anything extensive. This starts with a mindset to exercise; a mindset to endure the time of strengthening your heart and muscles, and burn off unwanted calories. You must endure the pain and uncomfortable feeling so that you can see the results that you're aiming for in attaining your goal. Likewise, before you get into the regimen of having a devoted time with the Master, you will need to take some time to prepare yourself each day. This requires discipline, dedication, and your devoted time without distraction. You must have the mindset of being alone with God to be able to have an experience that will bring you to a closer relationship with HIM. This means that you must shut yourself away from anything or anyone that will disturb, disrupt, or distract your reading and prayer time. Find a place in your home where you are free from all noise and clamor. It is recommended that you set a time in the morning before the regular time that you would prepare yourself and your family for the day. Make sure that this area is considered a do not disturb (DND) zone. Let your family or anyone that lives with you know that when they see you in that place, it is considered your "YOU TIME," and unless it is urgent, they must allow you that time to not be disturbed.

I'm reminded of the commercial of a woman that locked herself in the bathroom of her home, away from her family, just so that she could enjoy the pleasure of eating a cookie without interruption. Unfortunately, one of the toddlers called for mom on the other side of the locked door; however, to be able to reclaim her place of serenity, she deepened her voice and said with confidence, "its dad," in the hope that the naïve child would believe her and go away. Imagine the lengths that it took to first, escape from her family, especially the toddler to go into the bathroom without them noticing. Second, how did she manage to hide her favorite snack in a place that the curious toddler could not find? Thirdly, was that child missing her dad also that she went looking for mom? So much to consider in the commercial, but I bring this illustration to help you to understand the importance of going the extra mile to preserve your time to reach the goal of getting the encounter that you desire with God.

It may not be enough to just say "I'm having some "ME TIME"; you may have to go into your walk-in closet with a chair or reserve a space on the floor to get into what you are about to encounter on a daily basis. I recommend that you find some worship music to your liking to set the atmosphere. To ensure that you're not disturbing your family or others, purchase a set of headphones to attach to your device. Bring along with you your Bible, a journal, pen or pencil, highlighters and an expectation that you will receive an encounter with the Master! Although the devotional will have lines for you to write, you may need more space to jot down your experience. Everything that you experience will bring you into a deeper relationship with God. You don't want to leave anything out! There is a greater purpose for the experiences and encounters that you will have. Some experiences will be for the benefit of having a deeper understanding of who God is. Some experiences will thrust you into ministry. Some experiences will cause you to witness the grace and mercy of God to others that may desire to get closer to Him. Some experiences may cause a paradigm shift in your perspective on life itself; how you do things, say things, think of things and pray about things.

PRAYING TIME

Do you ever long to spend time talking and laughing with an old friend; someone that has known you for years? You can tell this person any and everything! You share your most vulnerable times, painful experiences, happy times, traumatic times as well as keeping up with "what happened throughout the day." You've become so close to this friend that you can call them anytime of the day and they will never complain, even if it's in the middle of the night when you can't sleep. What about those times that you had that major breakup with your then "special someone"? They were there to be that listening ear and that voice of reason and comfort, even though they told you in the beginning that they didn't think that person was for you. Nevertheless, they don't judge, but listen.

Beloved, we have just described to you the sincerest way of PRAYER! Allow me to ease the anxiety by stating that there is no specific tone or formula to talk with your FRIEND and Heavenly FATHER. He created you to have RELATIONSHIP with Him, not religious rituals. Some people don't pray because they compare their methods to someone else's way of expressing themselves in prayer. It doesn't mean that a person who will pray with a strong voice is any more powerful than someone that speaks with a soft, monotone voice. The power of the prayer comes from when you speak from your heart and become vulnerable to the One that has created you to commune with Him. The Bible expresses it this way, "God is spirit, and His worshipers must worship in the Spirit and in truth." (John 4:24)

Just like you would give reverence to your parents, you should do the same for your heavenly Father, the Creator of all things. He longs to spend time with you and hear all about the things that concern you. He is Omnipresent (always there), Omnipotent (all-seeing), and Omniscient (all-knowing), but like any good Father, he longs to hear your heart concerning your day-today matters. He also wants you to share your desires with Him, including the things that you tend to worry about. He says to 'come to Me, all who are weary and I will give you rest' (Matthew 11:28). Even if you feel ashamed, He is there for you to tell Him about your hurt, pain and discomfort. He acknowledges your tears and has compassion for you. He will listen and never expose you to others. He is truly a friend like no other. He's a safe place and refuge in times of trouble.

So, how do you get started? Let's consider the prayer model found in Matthew 6:9-13, as a flow of how we are to approach the throne of grace. Use the **R** to help you to remember each portion.

"Our Father, in heaven" – **R**everence Who He is.

"Hallowed be Your Name" – **R**eflect on God's sovereignty.

"Your Kingdom Come, your will be done on earth as it is in heaven" – **R**ender yourself as yielded to His word, will and ways by which He has purposed and planned for all.

"Give us this day our daily bread" – **R**equest your portion of provision for the day.

"Forgive us our debts, as we forgive our debtors" – **R**egpent of your sins and release those that have offended, hurt or caused pain towards you.

"And do not lead us into temptation, but deliver us from the evil one" – **R**emind God to make a way of escape from evil (sin).

"For yours is the kingdom and the power and the glory forever" – **R**efocus on the One that is all-powerful, all-knowing, all-seeing and in all places at all times.

"Amen" – **R**emain in the power of agreement with the Father.

IT'S A TIME OF FASTING

Joel 1:14

Consecrate a fast, call a sacred assembly; gather the elders and all the inhabitants of the land into the house of the Lord your God and cry out to the Lord.

Matthew 17:21

However, this kind does not go out except by prayer and fasting.

Fasting is a purposeful and voluntary act of abstaining from food or a pleasurable activity to focus your attention toward God. Fasting is also an effective response to challenging - physical or emotional - situations, circumstances, relationships and needs. In this case, it will help you to get clarity during your time of consecration while the focus is on you and your relationship with God.

In Scripture, fasting is almost always linked to abstaining from food. However, there are other ways to fast. Some may choose to abstain from sweets, television, social media and certain types of foods. You can consider fasting for a limited set time (I Corinthians 7:5), especially when the fasting is from food. Some may choose to fast from sun-up to sun-down. If you are on medications that require eating, you should not begin a fast from food, medicines or prescribed treatments without first consulting your physician. Some people may not be able to physically fast from food, but everyone can temporarily abstain from something to draw closer to God. He will accept it as your offering of sacrifice.

THREE TYPES OF FAST:

1. ***Normal Fast*** – To abstain from all forms of food and only drink water (Luke 4:1-2, Matthew 4:2-3, Genesis 24:33).

2. ***Absolute Fast or Total Fast*** – To abstain from all food as well as water. This type of fast can be extremely dangerous if not done

properly. Make sure that this is a fast that GOD has called you to do, and that it's not of yourself. This is a limited fast and should last for a maximum of 3 days (Acts 9:9, Ezra 10:6, Esther 4:16, Exodus 34:28, Deuteronomy 9:9, Deuteronomy 9:18).

3. *Partial Fast* – To abstain from certain foods such as meats, sweets, carbohydrates, etc. Or you may only eat certain types of foods like fruits, vegetables and whole grains (Daniel 1:12-15, Daniel 10:2-3, Matthew 3:4).

THE BENEFITS OF FASTING:

- ✓ Prepares the Penitent Heart – Joel 2:12-12-13.
- ✓ Adds Power for Spiritual Service – Matthew 17:21.
- ✓ Aids in Pursuing God – Daniel 9:3.
- ✓ Aids in Focusing on God – Joel 2:12.
- ✓ Rewarded When Done Discreetly – Matthew 6:16-18.
- ✓ Puts Us in a Posture of Humility – Psalm 35:13.
- ✓ Weapon in Spiritual Warfare – Esther 4:16.
- ✓ Sets the Captives Free – Isaiah 58:6.
- ✓ Ushers in Healing – Isaiah 58:8.
- ✓ Aids in receiving Direction – Acts 13:2.
- ✓ Gets Specific Prayers Answered – Ezra 8:23.
- ✓ Aids in Receiving Revelation – Daniel 9:3, 21-22.

The Anointing Oil Used for Consecration

Exodus 30:30-33 New King James Version (NKJV)

³⁰ And you shall anoint Aaron and his sons, and consecrate them, that *they* may minister to Me as priests. ³¹ "And you shall speak to the children of Israel, saying: 'This shall be a holy anointing oil to Me throughout your generations. ³² It shall not be poured on man's flesh; nor shall you make *any other* like it, according to its composition. It *is* holy, *and* it shall be holy to you. ³³ Whoever [a]compounds *any* like it, or whoever puts *any* of it on an outsider, shall be [b]cut off from his people.'"

As we focus on the scripture verses, we see that God gives specific instructions to His servant, Moses on how and why Aaron and his sons should be anointed with oil and consecrated for God's purpose. Because we serve a Holy GOD and everything that we dedicate to Him should be consecrated and set apart, not to be used for any worldly intention, He commands that the priests and the items that they would use be anointed with oil and consecrated for the sole purpose of relating to our Yahweh.

During your time of consecration, anointing yourself with anointing oil will become a part of your lifestyle while you purposely set your mind, heart and deeds toward God. Your focus during this time is considered holy and sacred. Some may not understand the significance of anointing yourself with the anointing oil before you start your day, but we will cover that information in this chapter. You may want to anoint yourself daily; as often as you pray; fast; or, at the beginning of your consecration week.

I have found that anointing yourself and praying sets the tone for your worship, praise and prayers of intercession. There is something about getting into the presence of God while having anointed yourself to be used as His conduit for the Holy Spirit to pray and make intercession. Of course, you don't fully know the needs of those in your community, cities, states or nations. But be assured, as you consecrate yourself to be used for the Master, He will give you utterances through prayer that may even shock you! This is the time that you dedicate yourself fully, dying to your fleshly desires, anointing yourself with fragranced oil so that it may be a sweet smell in the nostrils of our Holy God.

Exodus 28:41

"You shall anoint them, consecrate them and sanctify them, that they may minister to me as priests."

Matthew 6:17

"...when you fast, anoint your head..."

The anointing oils and the curated purpose:

- Frankincense: Intercession and healing.

    (Exodus 30:34-35)

- Myrrh: Purification, dying to self, peace.

    (Esther 2:12)

- Frankincense and Myrrh: Total victory and Lordship of the Messiah in spirit, soul [mind, will and emotions] and body.

- Hyssop: Cleansing, empowerment of the Holy Spirit.

    (Psalm 51:7)
- Cedars of Lebanon: Strength, performance, wholeness and restoration.

    (Psalm 92:12)

- Pomegranate: Fruitfulness, abundance, blessings and favor of God.

    (Song of Solomon 7:12)

- Spikenard: Intimacy and extravagant worship.
  (John 12:2-3)

- Cassia: Humility, servanthood, devotion.
  (Exodus 30:24)

- Rose of Sharon: Beauty of the Bride.
  (Song of Solomon 2:1)

- Covenant Oil:
  Covenantal relationship, marriage covenant.
  (Revelation 19:7-9)

- Cinnamon: Holy boldness, passion, courage.
  (Exodus 30)

- King's Garments (blend of myrrh, aloes and cassia): Glory, splendor and majesty of the King.
  (Psalm 45:8)

THE SOUNDS OF WORSHIP AND PRAISE

John 4:24

"God is spirit, and those who worship him must worship in spirit and truth."

2 Kings 3:15

"'But now bring me a musician.' And when the musician played, the hand of the LORD came upon him."

Music has a way of setting the atmosphere of the place[1] that you're in. When music is playing, your mind will focus on the tone, rhythm, and then the lyrics of the song. This will cause you to either move to the rhythm of the sound or become emotional, and sometimes, maybe even irritated if the lyrics and tones are intense. But in a time of worship, the music should pull you in and bring you into a place of rest and ease. The tones should be refreshing to your spirit, allowing your soul to be drawn into alignment so that the presence of God can arrest the atmosphere from any demonic activity (1 Sam 16:14-23). God is present when you are able to feel the fruits of His spirit (Galatians 5:22). It shall be like a sweet fragrance in His nostrils. At that moment, it is the time to minister to Him. Yes... tell Him how good and excellent He is. Speak well of His Name and attributes.

Psalm 45 (NKJV)

[1] My heart is overflowing with a good theme;
I recite my composition concerning the King;
My tongue is the pen of a ready writer.
[2] You are fairer than the sons of men;
Grace is poured upon Your lips;
Therefore, God has blessed You forever.
[3] Gird Your sword upon Your thigh, O Mighty One,
With Your glory and Your majesty.

⁴ And in Your majesty, ride prosperously because of truth,
humility, and righteousness;
And Your right hand shall teach You awesome things.
⁵ Your arrows are sharp in the heart of the King's enemies;
The peoples fall under You.
⁶ Your throne, O God, is forever and ever;
A scepter of righteousness is the scepter of Your kingdom.
⁷ You love righteousness and hate wickedness;
Therefore God, Your God, has anointed You
With the oil of gladness more than Your companions.
⁸ All Your garments are scented with myrrh and aloes and cassia,
Out of the ivory palaces, by which they have made You glad.
⁹ Kings' daughters are among Your honorable women;
At Your right hand stands the queen in gold from Ophir.
¹⁰ Listen, O daughter,
Consider and incline your ear;
Forget your own people also, and your father's house;
¹¹ So the King will greatly desire your beauty;
Because He is your Lord, worship Him.
¹² And the daughter of Tyre will come with a gift;
The rich among the people will seek your favor.
¹³ The royal daughter is all glorious within the palace;
Her clothing is woven with gold.
¹⁴ She shall be brought to the King in robes of many colors;
The virgins, her companions who follow her, shall be brought to
You.
¹⁵ With gladness and rejoicing, they shall be brought;
They shall enter the King's palace.
¹⁶ Instead of Your fathers shall be Your sons,
Whom You shall make princes in all the earth.
¹⁷ I will make Your name to be remembered in all generations;
Therefore, the people shall praise You forever and ever.

Reference the list of names of God below as your entry point of worship:

Name	Meaning	Reference
Jehovah	the self-existing one	*Genesis 2:4*
El Shaddai	God Almighty	*Genesis 28:3*
Jehovah-Roi	the God who sees	*Genesis 16:13*
Olam	the everlasting God	*Isaiah 40:28*
Adonai	Master or LORD	*Malachi 1:6*
Jehovah-Jireh	the LORD will provide	*Genesis 22:13,14*
Jehovah-Nissi	the LORD our banner	*Exodus 17:15*
Jehovah-Shalom	the LORD our peace	*Judges 6:24*
Jehovah-Sabaoth	the LORD of Hosts	*Isaiah 6:3*
Jehovah-Maccaddeschcem (M'Kaddesh)	the LORD my Sanctifier	*Exodus 31:13*
Jehovah-Ra`ah	the LORD my Shepherd	*Psalm 23:1*
Jehovah-Tsidkenu	the LORD our righteousness	*Jeremiah 23:6*
Jehovah-Shammah	the LORD Who is there	*Ezekiel 48:35*
Jehovah-Rapha	the LORD our healer	*Exodus 15:26*
Immanuel	God with us	*Isaiah 7:14*
El Yeshuw`ah	God is my salvation (Jesus)	*Isaiah 12:2*
El	God is my God	*Psalm 22:1,10*
Elohiym	God is my mighty creator	*Genesis 1:1*
Beyth-El	God is my sanctuary	*Genesis 31:13*
El Chay	God is my living truth	*Joshua 3:10*
Elyown (Elyon)	God is most high	*Genesis 14:18*

El Elohim	God is the only true God	*Daniel 11:36*
El Gamar	God is my God who works all things for me	*Psalm 57:2*
El Gibbowr (Gibor)	God is my mighty helper	*Isaiah 9:6*
Elohiym Yisra`el (Israel)	God is the God of Israel	*Exodus 5:1*
El Ro'iy (Roi)	God is all-seeing	*Genesis 16:13*
Elohiym Tehillah	God of my praise	*Psalm 109:1*
Elohiym Yasha`	God is my deliverer	*Psalm 80:7*
El Qanna	Jealous God	*Exodus 34:14*

*NOTE:
Soaking Music and songs of praise and worship are highly recommended during this time of consecration. You may find yourself kneeling in prayer; laying prostrate with your face to the ground; raising your hands and becoming very emotional. These are all normal during this time of reflection of Yahweh.

Take a moment to journal your thoughts of your worship experience here:

SUGGESTED MUSIC SELECTION

Worship Songs:

Music while journaling or meditating: Music To Journal by, ***Vol 1****,* ***Vol 2*** *or* ***Vol 3*** *Soaking Music by Julie True*

DAY 1 – *O Come to the Altar* by Elevation Collective (feat. Chris Brown, Mack Brock, Steven Furtick, Wade Joye).

DAY 2 – *You Say* by Lauren Daigle.

DAY 3 – *Nobody Like You Lord* by Miranda Curtis.

DAY 4 – *Indescribable* by Kierra Sheard.

DAY 5 – *Water* by Anthony Brown & Group Therapy.

DAY 6 – *Can't Even Imagine* by Desmond Pringle.

DAY 7 – *Still Believe* by Kim Walker-Smith.

DAY 8 – *You Know My Name* by Tasha Cobb-Leonard.

DAY 9 – *Bless Your Name* by All Nations Music.

DAY 10 – *Atmosphere Shift* by Jubilee Worship (feat. Phil Thompson).

DAY 11 – *Yahweh* by All Nations Music.

DAY 12 – *Majesty* by Gideon Band.

DAY 13 – *Can't Live Without You* by William McDowell.

DAY 14 – *There Is None Like You* by WorshipMob.

DAY 15 – *Jireh* by Elevation Worship & Maverick City (feat. Chandler Moore & Naomi Raine).

DAY 16 – *You Will Restore* by John Wilds.

DAY 17 – *Jesus Chainbreaker* by Chris House.

DAY 18 – *Redeemed* by Big Daddy Weave.

DAY 19 – *Good Father* by Chris Tomlin.

DAY 20 – *Alpha & Omega/God You're So Good* by WorshipMob (feat. Cross Worship).

DAY 21 – *The Blessing* by Melvin Crispell, III, Essential Worship (feat. Maranda Curtis).

**Please note that the song selection is only a recommendation, and may not align with your current time of consecration according to the suggested day. You may choose another music selection that will not only align with your place of consecration, but also minister to you as you listen.

YOUR MOUTH MATTERS

Key points to remember during your time of consecration.

1. God has given you authority in heaven and on earth (Job 22:28; Matthew 16:19).
    - All throughout Genesis 1, we find, "God said let there be…. And there was." In verse 26, we find that God said, "let US make man in OUR image, according to OUR likeness and have dominion." This affirms that just as God has spoken life and has dominion over creation, He has given us the same authority here on earth to speak to situations, and it shall be according to His will.
    - We have the authority to speak against the principalities, powers of darkness and spiritual wickedness that occur in the heavens.

    (Ephesians 6:12)

2. The words you speak have power (Proverbs 18:21).
    - Remember to speak only positive things concerning you, your family, and loved ones. No matter the situation, look in God's word to find a verse that speaks to that very situation. Put your name within the verse and pray it over yourself or others.
        - ✓ *Example: Psalm 1:1-3 "Blessed is (name) who does not walk in the counsel of the ungodly, nor stands in the path of sinners, nor sits in the seat of the scornful; But (name) delight is the law of the Lord, and in His law (name) meditates day and night. (Name) shall be like a tree planted by the rivers of water, that brings forth (his/her) fruit in (his/her) season, and (name) leaf also shall not wither; and whatever (he/she) does shall prosper."*

- During this time, be careful to speak words that spring a well of living water for those that may be thirsty to hear from God. You have the power to speak life into a dead situation (Ezekiel 37:1-14).

- God can use **you** as His vessel to encourage someone that may be having a challenge and need a ray of hope. Hope can be found in the words of encouragement that you speak over their life (Matthew 11:28-30; Romans 5:5; Romans 15:13).

3. Be quick to listen, slow to speak and slow to become angry (James 1:19).
   - There are 3 focuses here:
     a. **Listen:** Give one's attention; take notice of and act on what someone says.
     b. **Speak:** Say something in order to convey information, an opinion, or a feeling.
     c. **Angry:** Having a strong feeling of or showing annoyance, displeasure, or hostility.
        - ✓ *I like to demonstrate it this way: If you take the time to not only listen, but hear what the person is saying, you can speak to the topic without getting angry.*

   - There must be a pause in your being to allow someone to share situations with you without becoming judgmental or having a bias with a preconceived notion of what the other is going to say. Remove all walls, defenses and barriers that will prohibit you from listening to the person speaking.
     - ✓ *That includes your body language. The following are key points to note during such conversations:*
       a. *Unfolded arms reflect invitation.*
       b. *A smile on your face reflects that now is a good time to have a conversation.*

  c. *Inviting the person to sit reflects no partiality or judgement; you're both equal.*
  d. *Offering coffee or tea reflects a time to relax; fellowship is good at that moment.*

- Listening and hearing are two different concepts. You can listen to a song without hearing the lyrics. If your focus is on the rhythm of the music and the tone, you can totally miss the lyrics and the meaning of the message to the song. Hearing requires you to pay close attention to what is being said. Sometimes, you may even hear what isn't being spoken verbally, but emotionally, which is just as important. Always ask the Holy Spirit to speak as you humble yourself to be used as His vessel. He will reveal the unspoken words!

4. There are times that you must remain silent and not speak [pray] (Ecclesiastes 3:7b).
    - Get familiar with your seasons:
      a. Spring: Things are lovely, and new things are becoming into being. Though storms come, they are only there to help bring forth what has been planted.
      b. Summer: Everything is fine and you're loving life.
      c. Autumn: Things are beginning to change, and it doesn't look like life is perfect anymore. But you look at things from a new perspective, with a ray of hope that things aren't as they appear.
      d. Winter: It's cold, and you begin to feel as if you need to isolate yourself. Sometimes, things will be hard, and you need guidance on how to endure when nothing seems to be going your way.

    - There are times when it's just not a good time to speak to a situation, especially when you're going through your Winter. I suggest that is the time that you remain silent, if you are very emotional. Things have a way to

be misunderstood and not received in the manner that will be beneficial for others. However, that is the perfect time to seek the face of God for wisdom and understanding (James 1:5).
- Wait before speaking and addressing tough topics. Pray first and ask the Holy Spirit to give you the words that will bring healing, deliverance, encouragement, and comfort, so that God is glorified.

THE ALTAR CALL

Before going into the 21 Days of Consecration, let's talk about your spiritual walk with God – Yahweh, as we know Him. He is referred by many Names, such as Jehovah, Elohim, El-Shaddai, just to name a few.

Can you recall a date/time that you have had an opportunity to accept Jesus Christ as your personal Lord and Savior? Have you confessed with your mouth and believed with your heart that Jesus died, was buried and arose again for your sins? If not, let's establish a relationship through the gift of salvation. The following scriptures will lead us through what we call the Romans' Road to salvation. Read each, as we lead you to the place where you can be assured that when you leave this life of mortality, your soul will gain immortality in heaven.

Problem (sin):

- Romans 3:10 - "As it is written: 'there is none righteous, no not one.'"
- Romans 3:23 - "For all have sinned and fall short of the glory of God."

Penalty (death):

- Romans 5:12 - "Therefore, just as through one man, sin entered the world, and death through sin, and thus death spread to all men, because all sinned…"
- Romans 6:23a - "For the wages of sin is death."

Provision (Jesus' death):

- Romans 5:8 - "But God demonstrates His own love toward us, in that, while we were still sinners, Christ died for us."
- Romans 6:23b - "But the gift of God is eternal life in Christ Jesus our Lord."

Promise (salvation):

- Romans 10:9-10 [9]"that if you confess with your mouth the Lord Jesus and believe in your heart that God has raised Him from the dead, you will be saved. [10] For with the heart, one believes unto righteousness, and with the mouth, confession is made unto salvation."
- Romans 10:13 "For whoever calls on the name of the Lord shall be saved."

Sinner's Prayer *(Read aloud as your confession of faith)*

Jesus Christ, I acknowledge that I am a sinner in need of a Savior. I ask that you forgive me of my sins and create in me a clean heart. I ask that you come into my heart and use me to please You. I confess with my mouth and believe in my heart that You, Jesus died, was buried and rose again for my sins. I ask that you be Lord in my life as my Savior. I confess that I am redeemed through the power of the Holy Spirit. With the power of agreement of Your desire for my life, I AM SAVED!

CONGRATULATIONS ON YOUR NEW BIRTH THROUGH SALVATION!

YOUR NEW BIRTH DATE: _____ (date that you accepted Jesus as Savior and Lord).

From this moment forward, it is imperative that you know the following:

1. *Who you are* in the kingdom of God.

   - You are a new creation and no longer the old person. – 2 Corinthians 5:17-21

2. *Whose you are* in the kingdom of God.

- You are now a child of God; His very elect. He calls you a royal priesthood, a holy nation, joint heir with Christ. – 1 Peter 2:9-10

3. *What your rightful position* is in the kingdom of God.

   - You have the authority through Jesus Christ to bind (tie up) a demonic force and loose (release) God's blessings through your petitions (prayer) to God. – Matthew 16:19

**Pray that God will lead you to a faith-based community of believers (Church) that you can unite with for weekly service of worship, praise, prayer and Bible study. This will keep you encouraged and inspired as you grow in your spiritual journey. This assembly should be one that teaches from the Holy Bible as the final authority of your life. – Hebrews 10:24-25;
2 Timothy 3:16-17

REDEDICATION OF LIFE IN CHRIST

Jeremiah 3:14

*"Return, O backsliding children," says the L*ORD*; "for I am married to you. I will take you, one from a city and two from a family, and I will bring you to Zion." [NKJV]*

1 John 1:9

"If we confess our sins, He is faithful and just to forgive us our sins and to cleanse us from all unrighteousness." [NKJV]

Have you left your first love? Have you stopped reading your Bible? Have you started living life like you did prior to accepting Christ as your Lord and Savior? Where did your zeal to tell others about Christ go? When did you lose your desire to sit and be alone in His presence? Beloved, if you've done some self-reflection and realized that this is you, now would be a great time to rededicate your life to the Lord. He has called you into the Kingdom of God to be a representative of Jesus Christ. He has set you apart to be a light to a dark world. You are to be the salt of the earth. Beloved, the enemy comes to steal, kill and destroy God's very elect. He would love nothing more than to steal your joy, kill you spiritually while destroying your name and reputation. The enemy's strategy is to hinder your relationship with God; distract you from your God-given purpose; and, thwart the plans that God has for your life to get you to your destiny. If you recognize this activity in your life, I want you to repeat this scripture declaration:

NO WEAPON FORMED AGAINST ME SHALL PROSPER, AND EVERY TONGUE RISEN AGAINST ME IN JUDGEMENT, GOD SHALL CONDEMN. THIS IS THE HERITANCE THAT GOD HAS GIVEN ME IN RIGHTEOUSNESS!

Now, it is time to rededicate your life and life journey back to God.

1. Recognize your sinful posture that has distracted you from your devotion to God.
2. Renounce any type of ungodly activity (drinking of alcohol to get drunk; drugs with the intent to get high; fornication; adultery; and the like).
3. Repent [Godly sorrow, turn completely away from] of your sins (be specific, without using the phrase "if I did or done anything…").
4. Return your ways to God.
    a. Have quiet time in prayer and fasting.
    b. Start a daily devotional plan.
    c. Start journaling your thoughts and what God says to you.
    d. Surround yourself with other Christian people that are like-minded.
    e. Return to your church home service (faithfully), including:
        i. *Bible study.*
        ii. *Sunday School.*
        iii. *Christian Focus Studies.*

UNSURE OF SALVATION

1 John 5:13

"These things I have written to you who believe in the name of the Son of God, that you may know that you have eternal life, and that you may continue to believe in the name of the Son of God."

Hebrews 7:26-27

^{26} For such a High Priest was fitting for us, who is holy, harmless, undefiled, separate from sinners, and has become higher than the heavens; ^{27} who does not need daily, as those high priests, to offer up sacrifices, first for His own sins, and then for the people's, for this He did once, when He offered up Himself.

If you are unsure that you are saved through the gift of salvation, please be assured that once you have accepted Jesus Christ as Lord and Savior, you will spend eternity in heaven with our Father. Jesus died once and for all! Nothing that you can do will be able to separate you from the Father's love (Romans 8:37-39). If you have accepted Jesus Christ as Lord and Savior, it means that you have believed in your heart and confessed with your mouth that Jesus died, was buried and rose again for your sins. Therefore, YOU ARE SAVED!

21-DAY CONSECRATION

SET APART FOR THE MASTER'S USE DEVOTIONAL

LET'S BE RECONCILED!
Isaiah 1:18

e all have done things during our salvation that do not look like God, feel like God or speak like God. We have all disappointed Him by our actions, deeds, thoughts and words spoken. Whether good, bad or different, God still beckons us to come and be reconciled with Him. This means that we have to get back in the right posture with Him to look like, act like and speak like our heavenly Father. So then, what is your heart posture? Is it turned inward to self-gratification; outward to the things of this world; downward in oppression, suppression or depression; or upward, toward the hills which comes your help? How do you know which posture your heart is in? Examine the words that you release from your mouth, for out of it flows what is in your heart (Matthew 15:18). You can try to be "righteous" by your works, but even that is not good enough. The Bible speaks explicitly that even our righteousness is as filthy rags (Isa. 64:6); our hearts are deceitfully wicked (Genesis 6:5); and there is no good thing in this flesh. Paul tells us that all have sinned and fallen short of the glory of God, and as a result, death should be our portion (Romans 3:23; 6:23a). However, there is good news!!! Our newborn DNA reflects that our sinful blood is now covered under the sanctified blood of Jesus Christ. You have been purified, sanctified and justified by Jesus' death, burial and resurrection. For this reason, we are no longer called servants, but friends and joint heirs with Jesus Christ, our Savior (John 15:15). This is the time that we turn away from the sinful things that cause us to be separated from our Daddy. He is calling for us to get back to a place of consecration. He said that He is married to the backslider (Jeremiah 3:14). Come... let's be reconciled!

Journal what God is saying to you concerning this?

_____
_____
_____
_____
_____
_____
_____
_____
_____
_____
_____

What is your response?

_____
_____
_____
_____
_____
_____
_____
_____
_____
_____

Anoint Yourself... Which oil is God speaking for you to use for today?

Why?

Fast... What are you refraining from and taking time to seek God's face instead?

Journal your prayer here:

WHAT DOES IT MEAN TO BE CONSECRATED?
1 Peter 1:13-16

Consecration means to be set apart; separated; prepared and purposed to be used by God. It is imperative to know that you were born with a purpose in mind, and God's plans for you shall be fulfilled. You may feel like you have never fit in with others while growing up, although you've tried on so many levels. You may have been a loner most of your life; not that you wanted to be, it just happened that way. Sometimes, it might feel like you are alone, even in the midst of a crowd of people. You are so different and unique; but to some, strange at the same time (LOL). People don't like you for absolutely no reason at all; or so you think! OR, people love you as a person and they come to you for advice, but you won't be invited to the party! Your job is not just your job; it's your assignment. There is something that God has called you to do there and once it's done, on to the next "job." Not that you've planned to leave; someone just calls you out of the blue and offers you a position that gives you peace and you say yes to what you don't realize is your next assignment. There are undeniable times that the Lord will pull you away for a period of time, unexpectedly, just to be alone with Him. You wake up in the middle of the night and hear that still, small voice telling you things that is revelation knowledge, guidance, a word of wisdom, or just telling you to pray. Maybe this happens while you're in the shower or in the car alone, going to work. No radio playing… just quiet time, free of noise and distractions. You would love to eat lunch with co-workers, but you're prompted to read your Bible or some type of Christian material that heightens your spiritual curiosity. If this sounds familiar, take joy and be glad!!! God has separated you for an assignment that will make a difference in a dark place in this world. Rely on Him to show you purpose by design. Be sure to always be your authentic YOU… Just as He created you; never pretending to be someone other than how He purposed you to be. Remind yourself of this; if He created and consecrated me for a purpose, I can't be used if He doesn't recognize the image that He sees! Yep… this is what it means to be consecrated!

Journal what God is saying to you concerning this?

_____
_____
_____
_____
_____
_____
_____
_____
_____
_____

What is your response?

_____
_____
_____
_____
_____
_____
_____
_____

Anoint Yourself... Which oil is God speaking for you to use for today?

Why?

Fast… What are you refraining from and taking time to seek God's face instead?

Journal your prayer here:

CONSECRATED AND APPOINTED PRIEST
Leviticus 8:1-12

When God gave Moses specific instructions to show the people of Israel of what it means to be consecrated (set apart, separated) and anointed for God's purpose, he brought a natural demonstration to bring an understanding of what was happening in the spirit. This would also be a foreshadow of the matchless work that Jesus would do for the redemption of sin. It was indeed a new beginning for Aaron and his sons, as Moses would take and bathe them to indicate Yahweh cleansing them of sin and preparing them for priesthood. Moses was given the instruction to clothe Aaron with specific articles; a tunic, a sash, a robe, an ephod, a jeweled breastplate that represented the twelve tribes of Israel and a turban with an insignia on his head. Aaron would become the priest that would come to the altar on behalf of the people of Israel for forgiveness of their sins. Isn't it amazing how God would use a reflection of the garments of the priests to bring us to the understanding of what Paul mentioned in Ephesians 6:10-17 – to be fully clothed with our spiritual armor to fight against Satan and his ploys? As a priest praying and interceding on behalf of others, each piece of garment is like that of the armor. Your turban (helmet of salvation) with the insignia of Whose you are; the jeweled breastplate (breastplate of righteousness, confessing your sins and being an intercessor for the sins of others); sash (belt of truth) which pulls the garments together and enables you to carry your weapon); and a robe (which is your covering and garment of praise). You, as a priest of God, have been consecrated and purposed for the Master's use. You have been cleansed by the blood of Jesus and have on new garments with an insignia on your head to indicate to the world that you have been placed, purposed and prepared for the Master's use!

Journal what God is saying to you concerning this?

_____
_____
_____
_____
_____
_____
_____
_____
_____
_____

What is your response?

_____
_____
_____
_____
_____
_____
_____
_____

Anoint Yourself… Which oil is God speaking for you to use for today?

Why?

Fast… What are you refraining from and taking time to seek God's face instead?

Journal your prayer here:

CONSECRATED NOT COMPENSATED!
Mark 8:34-38

Consecration, in its finest, can appear to be a lonely place in time. There are people that you can't entertain, places that you can't go and things that you can't listen to or watch. The grace that God gives to some, He doesn't give to those that He has purposed for His use. You can't afford to lose your integrity and character for 5-15 minutes of worldly pleasure. Remember, the purpose of your consecration is to glorify your Father in Heaven. Unfortunately, but fortunately, you will lose the attention of associates, family members and co-workers to be in the right relationship with our heavenly Father. Notice that I mentioned "associates," not friends. True friends are always there for you without judgement (Prov 17:17). So, during your time of consecration, there may be times of separation from your friends, so that you will have more time with God and His word to prepare you for a new season in your life. There may also be a job opportunity that sounds very good, and the financial compensation may be very tempting. Your friends may encourage you to take the job because of the benefits and the pay. But, if that job is not the assignment that God has called you to, you must turn it down!!! Beloved, every opened door is not for you go through!! It may actually be a distraction from the place that God is assigning you to. You will know the one for you because the opportunity will bring peace to your spirit. You won't be compensated by man for your walk of obedience to what the Lord is calling you to do. But be glad and rejoice, beloved, that you shall receive the crown of life when you get to heaven for the work you've done here on earth. Don't you want to hear Him say, "Well done, my good and faithful servant"? You are consecrated, not compensated by man, but by God Himself!!!

Journal what God is saying to you concerning this?

_____
_____
_____
_____
_____
_____
_____
_____
_____
_____

What is your response?

_____
_____
_____
_____
_____
_____
_____
_____

Anoint Yourself… Which oil is God speaking for you to use for today?

Why?

Fast… What are you refraining from and taking time to seek God's face instead?

Journal your prayer here:

GOD'S ANOINTED AND APPOINTED
1 Samuel 16:13

Who God consecrates, He also anoints and appoints! God told Samuel to go to Jesse's house and there, find the one that he was to anoint as king over Israel. God appointed Himself a king that was among Jesse's sons. How special is that? That God chose one for Himself as king! When Samuel went to Jesse's house as instructed, he asked for Jesse to bring out *all* of his sons before him, that he may anoint the one that God had chosen as king. Jesse brought out the sons as directed. There, Samuel would consecrate them before seeking God's directive of who He had chosen as king. Jesse's sons were trained and skilled; they had the appearance of what the king should look like. However, God didn't choose the first one that appeared to be *the one* because God looks at the heart of man, not the outward appearance, nor the learned and skilled – as man does. Seven sons were brought out that others would consider qualified and capable to take on the assignment as king, but after no one was selected by God, Samuel asked if there was one being withheld among the sons. There was one that was neither skilled, nor trained; neither had he learned of kingship. He, in fact, was out in the fields, tending to sheep. A shepherd boy was called in without consecration, smelling of the stench of the fields, and dirty from the clay of the earth. But he was God's chosen misfit king, hand-picked by God Himself. This tells us that it doesn't matter if you're still walking in the stench of your sins and haven't been cleaned up for service. Whether you have a college degree/high school diploma or not, if you're God's chosen, He will anoint and appoint you for His service. Come as you are and wait for your appointed time. You are God's anointed and appointed!

Journal what God is saying to you concerning this?

_____
_____
_____
_____
_____
_____
_____
_____
_____
_____

What is your response?

_____
_____
_____
_____
_____
_____
_____
_____

Anoint Yourself… Which oil is God speaking for you to use for today?

Why?

Fast... What are you refraining from and taking time to seek God's face instead?

Journal your prayer here:

I HAVE NEED OF YOU......

Isaiah 6:1-8

Many are challenged with thinking that God cannot use us because of our past sins, addictions or ungodly habits. However, God chooses the least likely to be used by Him. Why is this, you may ask? It is because He knows our very being; our failures and shortcomings. He created you, knowing that you would make choices that are not pleasing to Him; speak things that do not align with His Word or His character; and make promises that you cannot keep! For this reason, God includes every type of failure and remedy in the Bible. To every problem, failure, as well as accomplishments, God has an outcome that reflects His grace and His mercy. This brings to mind the genealogy of Jesus, where His human lineage included murder, adultery, prostitution, incest and much more that we think can never be forgiven.

When God created you, He created you as part of His strategy to defeat the enemy. The Bible says, the gifts and callings of God are without repentance (Romans 11:29). Your gifts and calling are all part of the strategy that aligns with the purpose for your life. The very things that you believe to be hindrances are the things that God uses to keep you humble, compassionate and empathetic of others. He sends *you* to minister to the world about the love, grace and mercy that He has shown to all, including you. Isaiah was in the very presence of the HOLY GOD and immediately knew that he was going to die because of his sinful ways. But God didn't kill him; He petitioned him to come, by asking, "Who will go for us?" Isaiah used that opportunity to allow God to use him by responding, "Here I am...I'll go." God has need of you... will you go?

Journal what God is saying to you concerning this?

_____
_____
_____
_____
_____
_____
_____
_____
_____
_____

What is your response?

_____
_____
_____
_____
_____
_____
_____
_____

Anoint Yourself… Which oil is God speaking for you to use for today?

Why?

Fast... What are you refraining from and taking time to seek God's face instead?

Journal your prayer here:

I'VE CREATED YOU WITH A PURPOSE
Jeremiah 1:4-9

God called Jeremiah to use him even in his youthful years. Like most of us, we try to give God some excuse not to be used or not to fulfill the purpose that He has created us for; "Oh, but I am but a youth," meaning, "I'm too young…" or for some of you, "…too old for you to use me to speak to the people." God's response to Jeremiah was reassuring that He would be with him to lead him in what to say and the posture he was to hold. Just as God knew and created Jeremiah with a purpose, He has done the same with you! You, beloved, have a purpose and a destiny. When God created you, your life was already planned with an assignment attached to your name. He spoke to your spirit, and your very existence came to be in your mother's womb. The WORD that God spoke put a demand on your mother's womb and it had to obey. At that very moment, the vain of your existence put into action the strategy and responsibility of another human being to carry out His plan. You were formed, covered in secret, and nurtured until the manifestation of His word was birthed (Psalm 139:13-16). God said that His word would not return to Him void (Isaiah 55:11). That, beloved, means that you cannot be aborted, terminated or die until the manifestation of HIS word and your purpose has been fulfilled. Yes, with all of the things that you've done and the failures that you've had in your life, He has created you fulfill His ultimate plan. The truth is, God never allows anything in our lives to go without a purpose (Romans 8:28-29). He will ultimately get the glory out of the situation. Your mess will become your "message"; your test will become your "testimony"; and, your sad days will turn to your glad days. He will give you beauty for ashes and your latter will be greater than your past. You don't have to worry when God has given you an assignment for His glory. You are consecrated and created with a purpose!

Journal what God is saying to you concerning this?

_____
_____
_____
_____
_____
_____
_____
_____
_____
_____

What is your response?

_____
_____
_____
_____
_____
_____
_____
_____

Anoint Yourself… Which oil is God speaking for you to use for today?

Why?

Fast... What are you refraining from and taking time to seek God's face instead?

Journal your prayer here:

POWER IN THE PROMISE
2 Corinthians 1:20-21

Have you ever been in a position that God has told you that He was placing you in a position that you felt you weren't qualified or capable of doing for Him? Like, it appears to be so much greater than what you've ever seen yourself doing? Beloved, God has put a stamp of approval on your given position and assignment in the Kingdom of God. You have to know that it is Him that has affirmed and confirmed you! All that is required of you is to walk by faith and not by what you see. The power that is within you is motivated when you align your will to the will of what God has shown you. Be intentional about the things that are before you on a day-to-day basis in order for you to align with the purpose and the promise. Once you take a move forward, God will do the rest. The enemy's tactic is to make you doubt, get you frustrated and thus, get you to eventually quit! No matter what the enemy has tried to say or do to distract you from the promise that is within you, stand on the promise in God's Yes and Amen. His promise seals the deal because there is ***Power in the Promise***. So, when you begin to walk with confidence in God, you will find the power that is within you greater than what the enemy tries to bring against you. God's grace and the anointing for the position will keep you to complete the assignment that is on your life. Yes, the strategy and the weapon will be formed by the enemy, but it shall not prosper! God has risen up a standard against him! His tactics are limited, but you can do all things through Christ that strengthens you! Stand on His Word…Stand on His promises because there *is* **POWER IN THE PROMISE**!

Journal what God is saying to you concerning this?

_____
_____
_____
_____
_____
_____
_____
_____
_____

What is your response?

_____
_____
_____
_____
_____
_____
_____
_____

Anoint Yourself… Which oil is God speaking for you to use for today?

Why?

Fast... What are you refraining from and taking time to seek God's face instead?

Journal your prayer here:

YOU DON'T HAVE TO DO IT ALONE
Hebrews 13:5-6

There are times in ministry when we feel like, "If I don't do it, it won't get done." Beloved, that is far from the truth! That type of thought brings frustration, irritation, anxiety, fear, along with feeling of being overwhelmed. I don't know about you, but I surely don't want to do anything that will cause me to be stressed all the time! Those manifested characteristics are not from God, but the enemy! So, first ask yourself, "Was this assignment from God or from someone else, and I just took it on to please others?" Ah…. Here lies the rooted problem! If it was from someone else and you said yes without seeking God first, you've allowed yourself to do something that God did not assign or design for you to handle. This is how we can get in trouble, by allowing ourselves to please man out of fear of rejection or seeking affirmation. Beloved, when God gives an assignment, it comes with affirmation, confirmation, peace and effectiveness. Take the time to pray, and seek God for wisdom to go back and tell the person that you took on something without consulting God beforehand. Once you've done this, God will raise up the person that He has prepared to take on the task and complete it with excellence. Afterwards, you'll find that you've been released to focus on YOUR assignment that He has prepared, equipped and given you strategies to accomplish. He will divinely align others - that believe in the vision that God has given you - to assist. You don't have to do it alone! He is with you, guiding, leading and giving you wisdom to carry out the plan. You must allow Him to lead as you follow…it's a partnership! ***You don't have to do it alone!!!***

Journal what God is saying to you concerning this?

_____
_____
_____
_____
_____
_____
_____
_____
_____
_____
_____

What is your response?

_____
_____
_____
_____
_____
_____
_____
_____
_____

Anoint Yourself... Which oil is God speaking for you to use for today?

Why?

_____
_____
_____
_____
_____

Fast... What are you refraining from and taking time to seek God's face instead?

_____
_____

Journal your prayer here:

_____
_____
_____
_____
_____
_____
_____
_____
_____
_____
_____

STAND IN THE GAP

Isaiah 6:8

During your time of consecration, your prayer time should become more intentional. There are going to be times that you will be summoned through the Holy Spirit to open your mouth and use your voice as a weapon through intercession. As God's appointed ones, we are charged to not only go to God in prayer for guidance, direction and wisdom for ourselves, but He has also called us to pray and intercede on behalf of others. There are those that do not know that they can go directly to God about their situation or circumstances, but you do! God loves His children so much, that He will awaken you from your sleep at 2 or 3 o'clock in the morning to pray for someone else. It is in the stillness of the night, when no one else is around to distract or interrupt us that He will beckon us to pray. This is because we are so filled with our agendas throughout the day that we sometimes miss the opportunity to dialogue with the Father. So, God will awaken you from your slumber so that you can agree with Him and intercede for our family, friends, loved ones, co-laborers, those in authority over us, our disciples, co-workers and even our foes! Where there is a gap between the person and God, He will look for someone to stand in that space. Wake up!! You're in your season of consecration that's been set apart for the Master's use! Let's STAND IN THE GAP!!!

Journal what God is saying to you concerning this?

_____
_____
_____
_____
_____
_____
_____
_____
_____
_____

What is your response?

_____
_____
_____
_____
_____
_____
_____
_____

Anoint Yourself… Which oil is God speaking for you to use for today?

Why?

Fast... What are you refraining from and taking time to seek God's face instead?

Journal your prayer here:

THAT IS A DISTRACTION - STAY FOCUSED

1 Corinthians 7:35

Webster's Dictionary defines distraction in brief, as drawing apart; separation; confusion; perplexity; and, disorder. If you are going through any of those that I've just described, you, my dear are being distracted from Kingdom business! The enemy comes to steal, kill and destroy (John 10:10). One of the ways that he does this is to get your attention away from the assignment that God has given you, by causing you to focus on something else. It could be things happening at your workplace; your car is suddenly having issues; an issue with your finances, or a toxic relationship. The above-mentioned are examples of things that need your attention at some point. But I ask you, does the issue bring frustration, irritation, anger or worry? Or does it consume your thoughts throughout the day? If that is your dilemma, you are being distracted! God says to cast your cares on Him because He cares for you (1 Peter 5:7). The blessings of the Lord make one rich and adds not sorrow to it (Proverb 10:22). It doesn't mean that you will never have some challenges, but that these challenges should not hinder you from your God-given assignment. Take your eyes away from *that* and look to the hills from which comes your help. All of your help comes from the Lord (Psalm 121:2). Remember that God will never leave you nor forsake you. He has a track record; He has given you the victory in the past and He can do it again. He is Jehovah Jireh; He shall supply all of your needs according to His riches and glory. Tell Him about the problem and let Him handle it, while you handle the assignment that He has given you! You have to set a strategic plan of action to STAY FOCUSED because THAT (whatever your *"that"* is) is a DISTRACTION. First, recognize what your THAT is. Second, acknowledge that it is a DISTRACTION. Lastly, move on to what God has charged your hands to do…STAY FOCUSED!

Journal what God is saying to you concerning this?

_____
_____
_____
_____
_____
_____
_____
_____
_____
_____

What is your response?

_____
_____
_____
_____
_____
_____
_____
_____

Anoint Yourself… Which oil is God speaking for you to use for today?

Why?

Fast... What are you refraining from and taking time to seek God's face instead?

Journal your prayer here:

TOTAL OBEDIENCE
1 Samuel 15:22

You may have heard the saying, 'a little obedience is still disobedience.' That is true on many levels. If you find yourself telling someone a part of the story and leaving out a critical part of the story, that is deception, which is still considered a lie. You can't do one without doing all. The Bible says it this way, "a little leaven destroys the whole lump." Not part of the lump, but the entire lump. When we don't fully obey God and His instructions, we open ourselves to the hand of the enemy to deceive us and the consequences of that sin. Parents are given the responsibility to raise their children to learn to listen and obey. This daunting task is often combatted with a challenge and the power of the wills; the child wants to do it their way in spite of the guidance and instruction of their loving parents. The child doesn't give any thought to the fact that the parents are giving them instructions, not to hurt them, but for their own well-being. Likewise, we too, sometimes, struggle accepting the guidance or instruction of our Heavenly Father. For example, we may not understand why God wants us to apologize for something when we feel like we haven't done anything that warrants an apology to someone who has hurt us dearly. In fact, we believe that the offender should apologize to us! But God, in His Sovereignty, knows about the situation and requires us to humble ourselves and obey His command. In His infinite wisdom, He knows the end from the beginning and His instruction is for our well-being and to bring glory to Him. Who knows if our actions of obedience will cause others to draw closer to God, or release anger and hostility by speaking a kind word or giving a compassionate look with a smile? The outcome is God's responsibility. Our responsibility is to obey. For this reason, He is calling us to **obedience**.

Journal what God is saying to you concerning this?

_____
_____
_____
_____
_____
_____
_____
_____
_____
_____

What is your response?

_____
_____
_____
_____
_____
_____
_____
_____

Anoint Yourself... Which oil is God speaking for you to use for today?

Why?

Fast… What are you refraining from and taking time to seek God's face instead?

Journal your prayer here:

WHEN GOD IS SILENT?

Matthew 7:7

There are moments in every believer's journey through life when it appears as though God is silent. You are accustomed to hearing a response to your prayer through His audible voice, a scripture, a sermon or even through a conversation you're having with someone else, but this time, it's different. You have petitioned the Lord for guidance and an answer is warranted before making your next move. Have you considered that maybe He is waiting for you to make a move by faith, trusting that He will protect you and work everything out for your good? Sometimes, He wants us to trust Him enough to know that if it's a bad move on our part, He will protect us somehow from the circumstance that would follow. There is no failure in God, only victories and teachable moments [Rom. 8:28-29]. In saying this, you have been given the grace to seek and pursue His guidance by moving! Take a leap of faith and do something while you're waiting for Him to give the answer. After all, faith without works is dead! [Jas. 2:17] So, start the business plan and execute the strategy in pursuing your dream [Hab. 2:2]; start writing the book by getting a journal or tablet with pencils and jotting things down; start saving to purchase the home; apply for the job opportunity that will give you a pay increase and benefits. The point of the matter is, once you take the action to move forward by faith, you will see the manifestation of God's answer to your prayer. If you've asked, He will give you a YES, NO or WAIT, after you've initiated the move. If you seek His guidance after you've pursued the mission, He will reveal that it is His perfect will or His permissive will for you. Go for the perfect will; His permissive will can lead to disappointment and frustration. The Bible says, "The blessings of the Lord makes one rich and adds no sorrow to it" [Prov 10:22]. If you've gone toward a door of opportunity and the door is open, He is revealing that it is the way that you should go. He will open doors that no man can shut and close doors that no one can open [Rev 3:7]. He is waiting on you to do the walking and the talking, all while moving by faith. Trust that even when God is silent, He is still speaking!

Journal what God is saying to you concerning this?

_____
_____
_____
_____
_____
_____
_____
_____
_____
_____
_____

What is your response?

_____
_____
_____
_____
_____
_____
_____
_____
_____

Anoint Yourself... Which oil is God speaking for you to use for today?

Why?

Fast... What are you refraining from and taking time to seek God's face instead?

Journal your prayer here:

USE YOUR MANTLE

2 Kings 2:8

Have you gone to a place that God has led you to, only get there and feel stuck, or wonder, what next? You're facing an obstacle before you. You're certain that He has told you to go, but once you arrive, there are no further instructions; no manual; no voice from the Lord, telling you what to do next. At the very least, you're waiting for a confirmation! You can't move because you've reached the part of your journey that you've run out of options or it appears that you can't go any further. Others are following and watching you to see how you're maneuvering through an obstacle that is beyond your abilities. The place that you need to go is in your sight, but you haven't a clue as to how to maneuver toward the destination. Your answer is in your MANTLE! Your mantle happens to be your spiritual gift!! Your gift is that which the Holy Spirit has given you and requires you to use by faith to help you to reach your destiny! And also, to help others that are observing the path that they should take. No one truly knows the depth and power in which they carry until a demand has been put on it! How would you know that you are capable of speaking to the masses unless someone has asked you to speak to a few people in a group setting? You would never know the power of your words unless someone has asked you to pray for healing and the manifestation of healing has occurred. You would never know that your vision to start a company is lying dormant within you until you have lost your job! You have talents and gifts within you that require you to use the mantle in which God has given you to use in authority under the mighty hand of Jesus Christ! The word of God that has been spoken over your life cannot return to Him void! This means that you cannot die, unless every word spoken into the very vein of your existence has come to pass. This is accomplished by the mantle that you carry! So, USE YOUR MANTLE!!!

Journal what God is saying to you concerning this?

_____
_____
_____
_____
_____
_____
_____
_____
_____

What is your response?

_____
_____
_____
_____
_____
_____
_____
_____

Anoint Yourself… Which oil is God speaking for you to use for today?

Why?

_____
_____
_____
_____
_____

Fast... What are you refraining from and taking time to seek God's face instead?

_____
_____

Journal your prayer here:

_____
_____
_____
_____
_____
_____
_____
_____
_____
_____

GOD IS MY PORTION

Lamentations 3:24

Every day that we are graced to see another day, God provides us with a portion of what we will need to accomplish what is set before us. We do not know what the day will bring, but what we know for certain is that our Sovereign God is Omniscient (All-knowing), Omnipresent (At all places at all times), and Omnipotent (And All-seeing). He is the Alpha and the Omega; The Beginning and The End. He knows the ending of a matter before it begins. Our portion is whatever we need of Him for that day. If you are not feeling well, He is your Jehovah Rapha (God our Healer). If you have a financial need, He is your Jehovah Jireh (God our Provider). If there is something that is causing you to be weary, He is your Jehovah Shalom (God our Peace). Fighting a situation on your job? He is your Jehovah Sabaoth (The Lord of Host). The issue that some have is that they do not recognize the access we have at all times. Instead, we make our confessions based on our fleshly characteristics, instead of God's Holy attributes. When we confess sickness and claim it by the words "I am sick," we have come into alliance with the enemy to accept the ailment. Instead, we should confess the word of God by faith, that by Jesus' stripes, we are healed. Stand in the power of agreement with God and claim your portion of Jehovah Rapha for that day. Wisdom would have us to do what we can to overcome the issues of life by taking Western medicines, but while doing so, make your confession according to the word of God for deliverance, healing, and wholeness. Remember, we walk by faith and not by sight [2 Cor 5:7]. Faith without works is dead [Jas 2:17]. Without faith, it is impossible to please God [Heb 11:6]. Start today, confessing the attributes of God. Declare, "God is My Portion!"

Journal what God is saying to you concerning this?

_____
_____
_____
_____
_____
_____
_____
_____
_____

What is your response?

_____
_____
_____
_____
_____
_____
_____
_____

Anoint Yourself… Which oil is God speaking for you to use for today?

Why?

_____

_____

_____

_____

_____

_____

Fast... What are you refraining from and taking time to seek God's face instead?

_____

_____

Journal your prayer here:

_____

_____

_____

_____

_____

_____

_____

_____

_____

_____

_____

_____

IT'S TIME FOR BATTLE
LET'S GET DRESSED AND LET'S GO

> Remember:
>
> The battle is not yours, it's the lord's

2 Chronicles 20:15

"And he said, 'Listen, all you of Judah and you inhabitants of Jerusalem, and you, King Jehoshaphat! Thus says the LORD to you: Do not be afraid nor dismayed because of this great multitude, for the battle is not yours, but God's.'"

PUT YOUR GEAR ON!! (HELMET OF SALVATION)
Ephesians 6:10-17

No one would ever go into combat without the proper gear; fully dressed and ready for battle! One important piece of gear is the helmet to cover your head. That helmet has an insignia of the cross, which identifies which soldier that you represent in the battle. The mind, being the most critical part of your body, is where the battle begins. The things that we fight in our minds are spiritual. For example, the *spirit* of fear brings anxiety and can even paralyze you from moving and progressing toward success. It makes one think, "What if this happens or what if he/she doesn't like this or that?" when there is no evidence that conclude that "this or that" will occur. God does not give us a *spirit of fear*, but of power, love and a sound mind (2 Tim. 1:7). So then, we recognize that this spirit is not of God, but our adversary, Satan himself. As the child of God; blood-washed and heaven-bound, your strategic plan to survive a spiritual battle is to meditate on the Word of God. We must remember to "cast down arguments and every high thing that exalts itself against the knowledge of God, bringing every thought into captivity to the obedience of Christ" (1 Cor. 10:5). If the enemy can get you to think less of who God has called you to be, then he wins. There is power in the word of agreement! If you start to repeat that things that are contrary to God's word, you have then become an ally with the enemy! You have become a traitor against your own soul. Your salvation is so critical in spiritual warfare that the Lord says that one can chase 1000 and two can put 10,000 to flight (Deuteronomy 32:20a). You cannot afford to be a casualty on the battlefield. This gives you an opportunity to fight the thoughts of doubt, failure, suicide, depression, and oppression to get the victory over the enemy's tactics and win. When you thank God for the power of salvation through the death, burial and resurrection of Jesus Christ, you have already started winning the battle in spiritual warfare. Thank God for the power of salvation that keeps you covered through the blood of Christ Jesus. *PUT YOUR GEAR ON, STARTING WITH THE HELMET OF SALVATION!!!*

Journal what God is saying to you concerning this?

_____
_____
_____
_____
_____
_____
_____
_____
_____
_____

What is your response?

_____
_____
_____
_____
_____
_____
_____
_____
_____

Anoint Yourself... Which oil is God speaking for you to use for today?

Why?

Fast... What are you refraining from and taking time to seek God's face instead?

Journal your prayer here:

PUT YOUR GEAR ON!!
(BREASTPLATE OF RIGHTEOUSNESS)

Ephesians 6:10-17

The breastplate for the Roman soldiers covered the front and back of their torso. It fully covered the vital organs such as the lungs that enabled them to breathe; their kidneys that released the impurities from the body; and the heart that keeps the blood flowing throughout their veins. One pierce from a sword through the heart, the soldier dies from internal injuries. How significant is that? You can breathe with one lung; you can survive with one kidney, but one piercing of the heart, life ends as we know it. The Bible says that we should guard our hearts with all diligence. It goes on to say that what we have in our hearts is what comes out of our mouths (Proverbs 4:23). In Jeremiah 17:9-10, it tells us that the heart is deceitfully wicked, who can know it? God in His infinite power says that he does not consider the outer appearance of man, but He examines the heart of man. So, ask yourself, "What is in my heart? What types of conversations do I have with others? What are my motives of doing things that appear to be good?" Are your actions done to manipulate someone into doing something, when you have no control in the situation? It's time to do a heart check! As it is in the spirit, so it is in the natural. Spiritually - like our kidneys - we need to rid ourselves of the impurities of manipulation, control, bitterness, resentment and anger. We should breathe the breath of life in dead situations and allow our heart to be guarded from anything that will defile it. Love the unlovable; forgive even when they don't ask for forgiveness; give a positive response to a negative reaction; show them that our God lives! Life has a way of bringing things to us that can cause us to become emotional and act outside of our Christlike character. That is called HUMANITY! However, God already knows that "life" would occur and He has prepared a way of escape for you to get the victory. If you have done a heart check and found that there is wickedness, ask God to forgive you and seek healing. You will know that God is doing a work in you by the words that you speak and the actions that you display (Philippians 1:6). Protect your heart and PUT YOUR BREASTPLATE OF RIGHTOUSNESS ON!!!

Journal what God is saying to you concerning this?

_____
_____
_____
_____
_____
_____
_____
_____
_____

What is your response?

_____
_____
_____
_____
_____
_____
_____
_____

Anoint Yourself... Which oil is God speaking for you to use for today?

Why?

Fast… What are you refraining from and taking time to seek God's face instead?

Journal your prayer here:

PUT YOUR GEAR ON!! (BELT OF TRUTH)
Ephesians 6:10-17

When the Roman soldiers would prepare for battle, one piece of gear that they used to tighten the breastplate was a belt. The belt was intended to not only tighten the breastplate, but also to secure their sword and protect the reproductive organ that carried their seed. The belt of truth is tightened when you are able to protect your heart from defilement by reading your Bible; meditating on God's promises; and, memorizing scripture to speak truth when the enemy wants to kill you with a lie, or accusations concerning yourself or others. The problem that many of us have is that we don't stay in the truth enough, so, it becomes easy to dismiss "small" indiscretions that we make with excuses that - according to us - lessen the error. Unfortunately, that does not work, as it opposes the Word of truth. Anything that does not coincide with God's word is fallacy, and should not be overlooked, disregarded, or excused. As Shakespeare has stated, "To thine own-self, be true." It does you no good in your spiritual journey if you loosen your belt, lose your sword and allow your breastplate to become unsecured where mayhem and clumsiness can occur. What does that look like? The enemy will use situations, circumstances, and distractions to cause you to be double-minded. To be double-minded is to walk in accordance to God's word when all is going well, but react differently in times of trouble. You have to get a tight closure on the belt so that the enemy doesn't find a crack or opening in your garment and strike to kill your reputation, destroy your name and steal the joy of your salvation. Remember that the belt also covers the loins which reproduces your seed. Your seed represents your children that you are responsible to nurture, teach, protect, and govern over, and your ministry as well. Let's face facts, none of us are perfect, but we don't want the tactic of the enemy to create a more challenging scenario in our lives, sending darts that could possibly cause us to abort our mission! God wants us to win in every fight, battle, and war. But you can't do it if your belt is loose. PUT YOUR BELT OF TRUTH ON!!!

Journal what God is saying to you concerning this?

_____
_____
_____
_____
_____
_____
_____
_____
_____
_____

What is your response?

_____
_____
_____
_____
_____
_____
_____
_____

Anoint Yourself... Which oil is God speaking for you to use for today?

Why?

Fast... What are you refraining from and taking time to seek God's face instead?

Journal your prayer here:

PUT YOUR GEAR ON!! (GOSPEL SHOES)

Ephesians 6:10-17

A soldier must go into battle with the proper shoes to cover their feet. Their feet have to be properly covered and secured for three reasons:

1 – Without proper covering, the opponent is assured to get the upper hand if they step on your feet.

2 – Without the proper lacing, the shoes are able to come off of the foot, allowing you to lose ground.

3 – Without the proper soles, you are liable to fall; this also gives the opponent an advantage of killing and defeating you.

Can you imagine going into battle and fighting your opponent with the intent to get the victory, but your shoelaces have become undone? How can you run toward your enemy with a steady stride and come out of your shoes? What a catastrophe that will be; not only for you, but your comrades as well. Your mishap could be the casualty that the enemy needs to defeat your entire camp. As it is in the natural, so it is in the spirit. As the soldier of God's army, one of your responsibilities is to engage in warfare. You are selected to be on the front line of defense to keep your family protected. Your shoes are to secure your walk, that you may claim territory and break up fallow ground. The covering of the shoes is the anointing by which you have been given the authority to go into places and claim them as territory for the upbuilding of God's Kingdom. The laces of the shoes are to ensure that even when the enemy comes against you, you're not easily shaken and consequently, come undone. The soles of your shoes are to keep you grounded so that however the enemy pushes, you will be steadfast and unmovable. Get ready to march... PUT YOUR GOSPEL SHOES ON!!!

Journal what God is saying to you concerning this?

_____
_____
_____
_____
_____
_____
_____
_____
_____
_____

What is your response?

_____
_____
_____
_____
_____
_____
_____
_____
_____

Anoint Yourself… Which oil is God speaking for you to use for today?

Why?

Fast... What are you refraining from and taking time to seek God's face instead?

Journal your prayer here:

GET A GRIP!! (SHIELD OF FAITH)

Ephesians 6:10-17

Holding something in your hand requires you to use your palm, all four fingers and your thumb to secure the item without the potential of dropping it. To try to hold an object without this would not be very productive. However, the hand in its totality also requires the muscles, tendons, blood flow, bones, and the neurons from the brain to enable for such a task to be maneuvered with success. It will take all parts to be able to hold a cup of water, firmly grip a soda pop to open the cap or hold a sponge to bathe. When holding the shield of faith, it will take all mentioned elements to be able to move with procession against the enemy. Your adversary, Satan, does not fight fair and can cause you to stop moving toward your destiny according to the promise that God has purposed for your life, by sending fiery darts that is labeled "you can't do it," "you'll never be anything," "what if it doesn't work," "you're not qualified," "you're not the right size," "you're way out of your league," etc. All these are tactics of the enemy to discourage you from pursuing your dreams that will fulfill your purpose and propel you toward your destiny!!! You must have the faith to believe according to the Word of God, "I can do all things through Christ that strengthens me" [Phil 4:13], "For it is God who works in you both to will and to do for His good pleasure" [Phil 2:13], "I am fearfully and wonderfully made" [Psalms 139:14a], "I am God's chosen, a royal priesthood, a holy nation" [1 Pet 2:9]. The shield of faith is to block the fiery darts of the enemy so that it does not penetrate the soul (mind, will, emotions) because the adversary knows that if he can shoot a fiery dart that will penetrate your mind and emotions, it will alter your course of action through your will. Self-sabotage is part of the strategy of the enemy. You have the authority to pursue victory with a strategy of your own based on the word of God.

GET A GRIP!!!

Journal what God is saying to you concerning this?

_____
_____
_____
_____
_____
_____
_____
_____
_____
_____

What is your response?

_____
_____
_____
_____
_____
_____
_____
_____
_____
_____

Anoint Yourself… Which oil is God speaking for you to use for today?

Why?

_____
_____
_____
_____
_____

Fast... What are you refraining from and taking time to seek God's face instead?

_____
_____

Journal your prayer here:

_____
_____
_____
_____
_____
_____
_____
_____
_____
_____

GET A GRIP!! (SWORD OF THE SPIRIT)
Ephesians 6:10-17

As mentioned in the previous selection, *"holding something in your hand requires you to use your palm, all four fingers and your thumb to secure the item without the potential of dropping it. To try to hold an object without this would not be very productive. However, the hand in its totality also requires the muscles, tendons, blood flow, bones, and the neurons from the brain to enable for such a task to be maneuvered with success."* But here is when things can get a bit tricky! You have to move with coordination, using one hand to hold the shield of faith, while cutting the enemy with the SWORD OF THE SPIRIT!!! As a well-trained soldier, it is your duty and responsibility to pursue the enemy with the intent to win!! You have to be able to cut and divide what is truth against what is an untruth. The enemy shoots fiery darts that are sometimes mixed with deception, division, discord, and discouragement. How? Through gossip, presumptions, accusations, unresolved conflict, and abuse. We must remember that when we are faced with these types of devises, we should measure it by the Word of God, which is truth. This is part of the strategy that has been given to us to utilize as often as we ought. The Bible says, "For the word of God *is* living and powerful, and sharper than any two-edged sword, piercing even to the division of soul and spirit, and of joints and marrow, and is a discerner of the thoughts and intents of the heart" [Heb. 4:12]. Don't allow the enemy to gain ground over the Kingdom of God's territory by YOU coming against your own Christian brothers and sisters. He would like nothing more than to cause chaos in the Kingdom of God. The strategy weapon against that tactic is to quote, "How good and how pleasant it is for brethren (or sister) to dwell together in unity" [Ps. 133:1]. Also, memorize scripture and meditate on it day and night [Ps.1:2], so that when the enemy rushes in, you have your SWORD OF THE SPIRIT ready to engage in warfare and get the victory! GET A GRIP!!!

Journal what God is saying to you concerning this?

_____
_____
_____
_____
_____
_____
_____
_____
_____
_____

What is your response?

_____
_____
_____
_____
_____
_____
_____
_____
_____

Anoint Yourself… Which oil is God speaking for you to use for today?

Why?

Fast… What are you refraining from and taking time to seek God's face instead?

Journal your prayer here:

MINISTER KARON YARBOROUGH

BRIEF BIO

Minister Karon Yarborough, a Native D.C. Washingtonian; the biological mother of one adult son and daughter-in-love as well as the spiritual mother to many. She gained her education through the D.C. Public Schools.

Min. Karon has a passion for people and strongly desires for them to have an intimate relationship with God; empowering them to be strengthened in their spiritual walk with Christ; and, be ledby the Holy Spirit, is part of her mission and purpose in life. She has been commissioned by God to go and make disciples. Over a period of years, Min. Karon has discipled over 500 women that would empower them to make Christ the center of their lives and apply biblical principles that would embody the heart of Christ. This also leads her to teach and equip leaders to serve in their spiritual gifts for the upbuilding of God's Kingdom. This prompts her to teach Godly principles that encourages believers to growspiritually and have a more intimate relationship with Yahweh.

During Min. Karon's leisure time, she enjoys writing and is the author of the devotional book *"21-Day Consecration; Set Apart For The Master's Use."* Min. Karon was the RadioHost for the "Growing with Karon" live broadcast with WBGR Network and Co-Host of Podcast "Higher Heights".

She is a preacher, teacher and motivational speaker.

www.ingramcontent.com/pod-product-compliance
Lightning Source LLC
Chambersburg PA
CBHW071903070526
44583CB00016B/1828